CALIFORNIA LICENSE PRACTICE TEST QUESTIONS AND STUDY GUIDE

LEARN TO DRIVE SAFELY AND PASS THE WRITTEN TEST

2018

BY HANK WYSOCKI

COPYRIGHT © 2018 BY HANK WYSOCKI

TO LEARN MORE

www.driveredcoach.com

DISCLAIMER

INTRODUCTION

Many books and study guides have been written to help new drivers pass their written test. This book is very different in that is specifically designed not only to help you pass your written test the very first time, but also to help you learn and understand California State motor vehicle and traffic safety laws. Learning how to drive in a variety of traffic conditions as well as understanding road signs and modern defensive driving techniques will also be an intended outcome of this book.

This book is also very different in that is been written by a certified driver education Instructor who has taught in the classroom as well as on the road driving skills for over 34 years. The instructor has worked closely with DMV to make sure all student drivers understand driver and traffic safety laws specific to California. The instructor has more importantly stressed the importance of modern defensive driving techniques to all new drivers. The instructor understands how to teach the necessary skills in order to get young drivers out onto California State roads safely and defensively.

Statistics show that one in three first year drivers will be involved in a traffic collision. That it is why it is especially important to not only learn specific laws and rules that support driver and traffic safety, but also to reinforce these rules with plenty of practice on the vital techniques that make up successful defensive driving. As you go through this book it is not only important to take the time to learn the answers to the practice questions, but to also understand all the rules, laws and traffic signs that make up our highway transportation system.

It is also extremely important to seek out expert advice on how to drive safely and defensively. It is highly recommended that you enroll in a certified California Driver Education Program or at the very least take a few lessons from a professional driving instructor. This will help get you off to good start with essential defensive driving habits. Remember correcting bad habits later on is extremely difficult, so learn the correct way to drive at the very start of your driving career.

Want some help with learning how to drive correctly and defensively? Go to **www.driveredcoach.com** to get plenty of free information as well as a FREE guide to passing your California road test the first time. There are also two great books available on the topic of defensive driving and how to get started on the correct way to drive. Simply go to Amazon or click on the title to download these books. "Teach Your Teenager How to Drive a Car" or "Save Your Teenage Driver's Life."

WHY I WROTE THIS BOOK

This book was written to help new drivers pass their California Written Test the first time. It was also written to make sure new drivers understand the very important responsibility they have once they receive their license. Driving a 2000 pound vehicle is no joke. Please take the time as you go through the questions to not only comprehend why each answer is correct, but to also understand why you may have got it wrong. Your California driver's manual should serve as a valuable resource. The manual is over one hundred pages long and contains all of the necessary information related to driving a motor vehicle in the state of California. It is strongly recommended that you read this manual before embarking on these practice test questions. Getting your driver's license is a very exciting and rewarding phase of your life. Please take the necessary time to acquire all the essential information from the manual as well as this book. In addition, remember to also sign up for a California certified Driver Education Program or at the very least take a few professional driving lessons. Good luck and safe driving.

GETTING YOUR PERMIT IN CALIFORNIA

After you have studied your drivers' manual, and have taken the practice test questions in this book you are now ready to apply for your permit. On arrival to the DMV you will be asked to submit to an eye test, a fingerprint scan, and have your photograph taken. Next you will be asked to provide an application for your permit as well as several forms of Identification. A social security card, as well as another form of original proof of identity which includes date of birth is also required. Finally you will be asked to pay the appropriate permit fees to the DMV.

Once all of this has been accomplished you will be ready to take your written test. The test contains 46 multiple choice questions very similar to the ones you will study in this book. You must achieve a score of 36 correct questions or more in order to pass the exam. If you do not pass, don't worry you can take it over again. If you do pass, congratulations, you will receive your permit in the mail in approximately 2 weeks. This permit is valid for approximately 5 years. It is expected that you will sign up and take your road test before this permit expires.

Once you receive your permit it is important to get properly trained on how to drive defensively and safely. As we mentioned earlier in this book, sign up for a Driver Education program, get some professional lessons, and get a copy of a good book on modern driving procedures. Next order of business is to practice, practice, and more practice!

Good luck on your road test. If you should happen to pass remember that driving a car is a fluid process and that you will be continuing to learn your entire life. If you want some more great information on how to pass your road test the first time go to www.driveredcoach.com.

How this Book Is Organized

The California Driver's Manual is over 100 pages long. Fortunately you will not be tested on all 100 pages; however it is necessary that you take the time to look at and understand all of the other chapters. This book will be mainly concerned with the areas in the manual that you will be expected to know for your permit test.

Each chapter in this book will concentrate on a specific area of driving that you must understand to receive your permit, and eventually move on to receive your driver's license in California. You will notice that each chapter begins with some very important information that relates directly to California law and defensive driving tactics. Following this information, several practice test questions will follow to assist you with the knowledge of the topic. Immediately following these questions, the answers to these questions will be provided to give you immediate feedback. If you find yourself struggling on a specific topic (chapter) go back and read over that chapter in your California manual.

At the end of this book, a 46 question multiple choice test is provided, similar in structure to the one you will take for your permit test. The test questions will be based on the following topics: traffic controls, intersections and right of way, passing and being passed, defensive driving technique, alcohol and drugs, and sharing the road.

This book is designed to help you pass your permit test the first time. Read and understand the questions, and then answer the questions assigned to each topic. Once you have finished all the questions check your answers. If you get any questions wrong go back and check out why the appropriate answer was incorrect. After you go through the book once it may be necessary to go through all of the practice questions a second time to reinforce the correct responses.

Remember to use a copy of the updated California Driver's Manual as a primary resource when checking your answers. Good luck and happy studying!

ABOUT THE AUTHOR

Hank Wysocki has been a teacher, coach and administrator for over 34 years at the college, high school, and elementary school levels. He has taught driver education and defensive driving strategies to thousands of young students and adults throughout his career. Hank is a certified New York State Driver Education Teacher as well as an instructor of the Insurance and Point Reduction Program as an affiliate for

Driver Training Associates. He is an active advocate of parent involvement within the entire driver education process for new and beginning drivers. This book is the fourth publication in a series of educational resources designed by Hank Wysocki to help promote, and educate everyone on the strategies and techniques of defensive driving. Hank's intention is to help bridge the critical gap between parents and their teenage drivers.

If there is a private or public school driving instructor involved with your driver education be sure to reinforce the correct driving habits they teach as well as the information in this book each and every time you get behind the wheel. Also, be sure to get plenty of practice opportunities to complement these lessons. Sound, repeatable, positive habits should be molded early in the driving process. Destructive, life threatening habits are much more difficult to change later in life. Good luck and safe driving.

Connect with Hank at:

www.driveredcoach.com

www.facebook.com/driveredcoach

amazon.com/author/hankwysocki

TABLE OF CONTENTS

Chapter 1 Traffic Controls

The topic of traffic controls refers to all of the signs, lights, lines and pavement markings that regulate traffic on our nation's highways.

Roadway Signs

Roadway signs are categorized into four distinct groups. The groups are regulatory, warning, guide, service and recreation (destination) and construction. The color and shape also help to determine which group each sign belongs in.

Regulatory:

This group of signs reminds motorists of a traffic regulation. They are usually black and white or red in color. The majority of these signs are rectangular by nature, with the exception of the octagon shaped stop sign, and the down pointed triangle, yield sign.

Warning:

Warning signs alert motorists to an impending danger. These signs are yellow and black in color and are usually diamond shaped. School zone signs are pentagon shaped and railroad crossing signs are round.

GUIDE, SERVICE AND RECREATION (DESTINATION):

You will find this category of signs mainly on major highways and expressways throughout the country. The blue service signs make motorists aware of services that are available to them at certain exits. The green signs will help you get to your desired destination and the brown signs refer motorists to camping areas and historical sites.

CONSTRUCTION:

Construction signs alert driver's to an upcoming roadwork project. These signs are recognizable by their distinct orange color and are usually diamond shaped.

LINES AND PAVEMENT MARKINGS

Lines and pavement markings divide lanes, alert drivers to when it is safe to pass and are used for turns at traffic lights and signs.

EDGE MARKINGS

The markings on the edges of roads are white on a two direction of travel road. The edge marking on the right is white and the marking on the left is yellow for a one way road.

CENTER LINES

The color yellow in the middle of roadways represents a two way direction of travel road. The color white represents a one way roadway. Dotted lines allow for passing and double yellow lines do not. A single solid white line allows for a pass only when necessary and safe to do so.

CROSS WALKS AND STOP LINES

You must make your complete stop behind cross walks and stop lines before proceeding. If there is no cross walk or stop line, stop as close to the stop sign as possible where you can see traffic. Use the sidewalks on both sides of street as a reference point to stop.

TRAFFIC LIGHTS

Steady Red Light- Means you must make a complete stop, and wait for light to turn green.

Flashing Red Light- Same rule as a stop sign. Stop, look and yield right of way before proceeding.

Flashing Yellow Light- Proceed with caution.

Green Arrow- Represents a protected left turn.

Steady Green- Proceed but be sure to check traffic as you go through intersection.

Yellow Light- Cover brake and be ready to stop.

Traffic Officer- Takes precedence over all signs and lights. Always obey their directions first.

PRACTICE QUESTIONS CHAPTER 1
1. What does a pentagon shaped sign represent?
   a. Camping area
   b. School Zone
   c. Construction
   d. Speed Limit
2. Which of the following should be obeyed first?
   a. Stop sign
   b. Red Light
   c. Yield Sign
   d. Traffic Officer
3. What category of signs does a railroad crossing belong?
   a. Construction
   b. Destination
   c. Warning
   d. Regulatory
4. When may you cross a double solid yellow line?
   a. Never
   b. To pass a slow truck
   c. When traffic permits

d. To pass any slow moving vehicle

5. A yellow edge marking on the left side of the road represents?
   a. Two directions of travel
   b. Parking area
   c. One way road
   d. Construction zone

6. If a traffic signal is not functioning you should:
   a. Stop completely and proceed through intersection when safe
   b. Continue through the intersection
   c. Slow down only if necessary
   d. Yield right of way to all traffic

7. What should you do if a pedestrian is crossing street with no crosswalk?
   a. Slow down and pass the pedestrian
   b. Make eye contact with pedestrian and go around them
   c. Come to a complete stop and let pedestrian cross
   d. Pedestrian is jaywalking continue driving

8. When turning left on a green arrow you should:
   a. Wait 4 seconds before proceeding
   b. Yield the right of way to pedestrians only
   c. Yield the right of way to other vehicles, pedestrians and bicycles

d. You have right of way continue through the intersection

9. If you notice orange construction signs on a freeway you should:
   a. Change lanes and continue at same speed
   b. Just be aware of the workers ahead, keep your speed
   c. Be prepared to slow down or change lanes or both for the workers ahead
   d. No changes of speed or lane position required

10. A flashing yellow light requires you to:
    a. Stop completely
    b. Slow down and be cautious
    c. Make a protected left hand turn
    d. Pull over to right side of road

ANSWERS CHAPTER 1

1. A pentagon shape represents (b) a school zone. It is a warning sign and is yellow and black.
2. A traffic officer (d) has authority over all signs and lights.
3. A railroad crossing sign belongs in (c) warning category. It is circular shaped and is yellow and black.
4. You may never (a) cross a double yellow line.

5. A yellow edge marking on the left represents (c) a one way road. The right side edge marking is white on a one way road.
6. Stop completely and proceed when intersection is safe (a)
7. Completely stop and let the pedestrian cross (c)
8. Yield the right of way to vehicles, pedestrians and bicycles (c)
9. Be prepared to slow down, change lanes or both for workers ahead (c)
10. Slow down and be cautious for a yellow light (b)

CHAPTER 2 INTERSECTIONS, TURNING, AND RIGHT OF WAY

More than one third of all accidents occur at intersections. Using the effective defensive driving principles of *following distance* and *visual lead time* can go a long way in the prevention of an accident. It is also paramount that new driver's understand right of way rules in order to resolve certain driving conflicts. Here are some of the most important right of way rules:

1. Yield the right of way to pedestrians at all times!
2. Drivers must yield right of way to authorized emergency vehicles. Pull over and stop on the right hand side of the road to allow these vehicles to pass.
3. A vehicle in the intersection has the right of way over a vehicle preparing to enter. If the light turns red over your head you have the right of way to complete your turn.
4. A vehicle in a traffic circle has the right of way over a vehicle preparing to enter a traffic circle.
5. The car that reaches a four way stop has right of way over entering vehicles. When two cars reach a four way stop at the

same time the car on the right has the right of way.

6. A vehicle on a major roadway has the right of way over a vehicle preparing to enter from a driveway, alleyway or private roadway.

It is always a good idea to approach any intersection with caution. Make sure to cover your brake and always anticipate the worst.

ADVICE ON TURNING

1. Signal early! You should signal your intention to turn at least 100 feet before the intersection.

2. Keep your front end out when turning. The front end of your car that is. Remember your rear wheels do not *track* the same way as your front wheels. Keeping your front end out allows you to avoid driving over a curb. This principle also hold true when backing out of a parking space. Make sure you back up straight before beginning your turn in any parking lot.

3. When you make a left hand turn from a two direction of travel road into a four lane road, always make your turn into the lane closest to you.

4. Always make your turn in the lane closest to you when you turn from a one way road into a one way road. It is also the same procedure when turning from a two direction of travel road into a one way road. Turn into the lane closest to you.

5. When making any right hand turn stay as far right as possible and keep your front end out slightly to avoid running over the curb.

U Turns and Three Point Turns

Only use a u turn and a three point turn when it is absolutely necessary, and of course when it is legal. To perform a three point turn make sure you signal to the curb first and stop. Next be certain to signal away from curb, check your mirror and lastly check your blind spot. Crank your wheel all the way to the left and roll to the opposite curb. Stop short of the curb and shift to reverse. Crank the wheel clockwise as you look in the direction you are moving. Stop when you know you have enough clear space to complete the maneuver. Shift to drive and crank the steering wheel counter clockwise.

Practice Questions Chapter 2

1. Two cars arrive at a four way stop at the same time. Who has the right of way?

a. The car on the right.
b. The car on the left.
c. The car approaching the intersection.
d. The last car to arrive to the intersection.

2. You are entering a major roadway from an alleyway. You should:
   a. Accelerate and merge smoothly
   b. Pull into the road to block traffic
   c. Sound your horn and wait for someone to wave you in
   d. Yield right of way to all traffic and pedestrians

3. When turning left from a 2 way road into a 4 lane road. You should:
   a. Turn left into the lane closest to you
   b. Turn into the right hand lane
   c. Turn into the lane with the least traffic
   d. Turn into the center of the road

4. You hear a siren and notice lights flashing in your rear view mirror. You should:
   a. Slow down where you are and allow them to pass on the right
   b. Pull over to the right, stop and allow emergency vehicle to pass
   c. Speed up and get out of their way
   d. Pull over to the left hand side of road and stop

5. You are preparing to turn left at an unprotected intersection. You should:

a. Keep your wheels straight and wait for traffic to clear before turning
b. Make your turn traffic will get out of your way
c. Keep your wheels turned left and wait for traffic to clear before turning
d. Flash your lights and beep your horn so traffic will let you proceed

6. How many feet should you signal your intended turn?
   a. 500 feet
   b. 2000 feet
   c. 50 feet
   d. 100 feet

7. You may generally turn right on a red light when:
   a. There is no sign prohibiting it
   b. After a complete stop
   c. When there are no pedestrians or bicycle to obstruct your turn
   d. All of the above are correct

8. When can you perform a u turn in a residential district?
   a. When there are no cars approaching from the other side and no sign restricts
   b. Never
   c. Only on a one way road
   d. Across two sets of double yellow lines

9. When preparing to make a right turn at a corner you should:
   a. Merge into the bicycle lane before turning
   b. May never enter bicycle lane
   c. Make a wide turn around bicycle lane
   d. Continue on to the next corner
10. A solid yellow line on your side of center stripe means:
    a. Pass with caution
    b. Pass at any time
    c. You may turn any time
    d. You may turn when the intersection is clear

ANSWERS CHAPTER 2

1. The car on the right has the right of way (a). This is called the same time rule.
2. Alleyway, driveways and private roadways always yield right of way to the major road (d).
3. When making any left into a multi- lane roadway always make the turn in the lane closest to you (a).
4. Any time you hear a siren or see flashing lights pull over and stop on the right hand side of the road, and allow the emergency vehicle to pass on your left (b).
5. When you are waiting at an unprotected intersection (no green arrow) remember

to keep your wheels straight so that if you are hit from behind your car will not be sent into traffic. Make sure you have enough clear space before completing your turn (a).

6. You should activate your signal 100 feet before a turn (d).
7. All of the above is correct! (d)
8. A u turn may be accomplished when traffic is clear and no sign restricts (a).
9. Merge into the bicycle lane before turning (a).
10. You may only complete a turn on a yellow line when intersection is clear (d).

CHAPTER 3 PASSING AND BEING PASSED

The highway transportation system has been set up so that slower moving vehicles drive in the right hand lane and drivers that intend to pass will do so in the left hand lane. Continuous use of the right hand lane to pass other vehicles can upset this system and perhaps cause an accident. Passing on the right can be accomplished during the following circumstances:

1. On a multi-lane road in which passing (overtaking) on the right is not prohibited. Overtaking simply means going by a vehicle on the right without returning to left or center lane.
2. When a vehicle on your left is making a left hand turn.

One thing is for certain every pass should be made by first signaling your intent, second checking your mirrors and finally checking your blind spot. This is the proper protocol for any lateral maneuver. Passing on a two direction of travel road in which dotted yellow lines are located in the middle or on your side of the road present a very dangerous situation because of the potential of a head on collision. If you plan to pass in this situation you should always make sure that you:

1. Have enough clear space to make the pass.
2. The pass is absolutely necessary.
3. The car ahead is going slow enough to complete a legal pass.

When returning to your original lane after the pass it is always a good idea to see both headlights of the car you just passed before returning to your original lane.

SPECIAL SITUATIONS

California now has a move over law. All vehicles traveling on multi-lane roads need to move to the middle lane or at the very least slow down when a police vehicle or ambulance is pulled over on the right side of the highway. This law was also expanded for tow trucks and snow plows and many other construction vehicles pulled over to the right.

When a school bus is stopped and is flashing its red lights all vehicles should stop a minimum of 20 feet from that stopped bus. This action takes place for vehicles traveling in both directions. Once the red lights have stopped flashing you may proceed with caution.

Construction zones have become an extremely serious situation for our important road workers. Orange signs alert drivers to these impending work zones. Remember to slow down to the speed limit displayed by these signs and stay alert and scan the road for any problems in your driving path. Traffic fines double if you are pulled over for a construction zone violation.

PRACTICE TEST QUESTIONS CHAPTER 3

1. You may complete a pass (overtake) a vehicle on the right when:
   a. It is turning right
   b. Stopped in heavy traffic
   c. Parked on the side of road.
   d. It is turning left.
2. A school bus is stopped with red lights flashing. You should:
   a. Completely stop your vehicle at least 20 feet from the bus.
   b. Slow down and move cautiously around the bus
   c. Stop briefly then proceed
   d. Pass only if you are on the opposite side of the road
3. Once you have completed a pass of another vehicle it is safe to return to your lane when:
   a. See the other car slow down.

b. When the car you are passing sounds their horn

c. When the car you are passing slows down.

d. You can see the headlights of the car you are passing in your rear view mirror.

4. When is it safe to pass on a 2 lane highway?

a. When you have enough clear space

b. When you are going far enough to make the decision to pass worthwhile

c. When the car ahead is going slow enough to warrant a pass

d. All of the above

5. What should you do when another car is passing you?

a. Slow down slightly and remain in your lane

b. Speed up and stay in your lane

c. Beep your horn to alert driver that it is safe to return to the right lane

d. Pull over and stop to allow driver to pass you

6. What should you do if an emergency vehicle is on the shoulder of a freeway?

a. Continue in your lane making eye contact with responders

b. Move to the center lane

c. Move all the way to the left lane quickly

d. Move to shoulder to see if you can help

7. When can you go off the road to pass another vehicle?
   a. Only if a police officer instructs you to
   b. Only when turning left
   c. Only if your vehicle is designed for off road travel
   d. If the car ahead is going too slow

8. What should you do if you hear a siren of an emergency vehicle behind you?
   a. Pull over to the right side of the road
   b. Speed up to avoid the emergency vehicle
   c. Pull over to the left side of road
   d. Stay where you are and let the emergency vehicle go around you

9. Always look carefully for motorcycles when changing lanes because:
   a. They have the right of way on all roads
   b. They are difficult to see
   c. They may never share a lane
   d. They obey different traffic laws

10. When executing any pass you should:
    a. Signal, check your mirrors and check your blind spot in that order

b. Slow down and signal
c. Speed up and swerve around vehicle ahead
d. Just rely on your mirrors

ANSWERS CHAPTER 3

1. You may pass a vehicle on the right when they are turning left and if the pass is legal (d).
2. You need to stop completely at least 20 feet from the school bus when red lights are flashing (a).
3. It is safe to return to your lane after you pass once you see both headlights of the car you have passed in your rear view mirror (d).
4. One of the most dangerous passes is when you have cross dotted yellow lines on a 2 way road the correct answer is (d) all of the above.
5. When another car is passing you slow down slightly and remain in your lane (a).
6. You should move to the center lane to give space (b).
7. Only if a police officer instructs you to (a).
8. Pull over to the right and allow emergency vehicle to pass (a).
9. Motorcycles are difficult to see (b).

10. Always signal, check your mirror and your blind spot (a).

CHAPTER 4 DRIVING MANEUVERS

Once you attain a license to drive in California the two most common driving maneuvers that you will most likely use in your everyday driving are the skills of parallel parking and three point turns. Both of these skills will be tested on your California road test. It is important to not only know how to perform these skills, but is equally important to know when parking and certain change of direction turns are illegal.

THE THREE MUST MISUNDERSTOOD SIGNS

You will basically come in contact with three signs in California that are concerned with parking. They are:

1. No Stopping-No stopping means you may not stop in this area whatsoever.
2. No Parking-No parking means that you can load or unload packages or passengers temporarily.
3. No Standing-No standing means that you may load or unload passengers only and temporarily.

Another parking sign that you may see quite often is a reserved parking space for the disabled. It is illegal to park in these spaces unless you have a visible permit issued by the state, city, town or village.

One important sign to keep your eyes open for is a no U-Turn sign. Under no circumstances are you allowed to complete this maneuver when you see this sign.

How to Parallel Park

Step 1- Signal right and line up your side view mirrors with the car you are parking behind about 2-3 feet away.

Step 2- Crank your steering wheel all the way clockwise as you roll back slowly. Stop when the passenger seat is equal with the bumper.

Step 3- Straighten your tires by turning your steering wheel 1 to 1 ½ cranks.

Step 4- Roll back slowly with the tires straight and turn your steering wheel all the way counter clockwise as your front end just passes the bumper of the car you are parking behind.

Step 5- Turn your steering wheel clockwise and straighten your tires. Shift to drive and roll slowly forward continuing to straighten your tires.

During this maneuver it is very important to look over your right shoulder when going in reverse. It is also important to signal, check your mirrors and finally your blind spot when pulling away from the curb. When parking on a hill remember to set your parking brake and to turn your tires in a direction so that your vehicle will not head into traffic. If there is a curb, you can use the curb as a "backstop" by facing your tires away from the curb on an uphill and into the curb on a downhill.

THREE POINT TURN

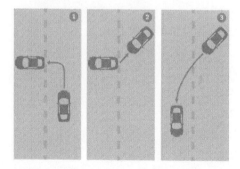

Step 1- Signal right and pull to the curb. Crank your wheels all the way counter clockwise, and roll forward to the opposite curb. Remember to signal, check your mirrors and finally your blind spot when leaving the curb.

Step 2- Shift to reverse and crank your wheel all the way clockwise, and roll back slowly as you look back over your right shoulder. Stop when you know you have enough clear space to complete the turn.

Step 3- Shift to drive and turn your steering wheel all the way counter clockwise. Roll forward to complete the maneuver.

PRACTICE TEST QUESTIONS CHAPTER 4

1. A no-standing sign means:
    a. You may unload packages temporarily.
    b. You may unload passengers temporarily.
    c. You may unload packages or passengers temporarily.
    d. You can never stop there.
2. Before leaving the curb on a three point turn you should:
    a. Signal, check your mirrors and finally make a blind spot check.
    b. Check your mirrors and go.
    c. Signal and go.
    d. Make the turn immediately to avoid blocking traffic.

3. At no time should you park:
    a. On a one way street

b. In a parking space at the store.

c. In front of a building.

d. On railroad tracks.

4. When can a driver without a disability park in a spot reserved for the disabled?

    a. May never park, stop or stand in this spot.

    b. During an emergency.

    c. Temporarily to drop off passengers.

    d. Temporarily to drop off packages.

5. Once you have completed a parallel park on level ground you should:

    a. Keep your tires pointed toward the road to exit easily.

    b. Move as close to the car behind you as possible.

    c. Just barely touch the bumper of the car in front of you.

    d. Leave equal space between both cars with your tires pointed straight.

ANSWERS CHAPTER 4

1. A no-standing sign means that you may unload passengers temporarily (b).

2. Before leaving the curb on a three point turn always remember to signal, check your mirrors and finally your blind spot (a). You should do this for all lateral maneuvers.

3. At no time should you park on railroad tracks (d). Other places include fire hydrants, cross walks, tunnels and bridges.
4. A non-disabled driver may never park, stand or stop in a parking spot reserved for disabled drivers (a).
5. Once you have completed your parallel park make sure your tires are pointed straight and you have equal space between both cars (d).

CHAPTER 5 DEFENSIVE DRIVING TECHNIQUE

Nearly 80% of all accidents that occur on our nation's highways are preventable. By simply learning a few defensive driving concepts and skills everyone can become a defensive driver. Defensive driving involves watching out for the "other guy" and never assuming they will do the right thing. SIPDE is the current system of defensive driving that is being taught to new drivers. Each letter in the acronym SIPDE represents an important concept that everyone needs to understand in order to drive defensively.

Search ahead by using a good visual lead time, looking for anything that may cause a problem to you well in advance.

Identify these problems in your path of travel.

Predict how these problems could affect your driving.

Decide what you need to do to prevent a possible collision.

Execute the decision that you have made.

Remember that everyone who drives a motor vehicle has three important controls of their car, braking, steering and acceleration. By simply using the concept of SIPDE in combination with the three car controls, accidents can be dramatically reduced. It is also important to always drive with a following distance behind another vehicle. This following distance gives you a nice cushion just in case the vehicle ahead brakes abruptly or you take your eyes off the road for a brief second. Defensive driving also involves obeying and understanding the laws and rules of the road. It also involves wearing a safety belt just in case you are involved in a collision.

SPEED

Regulatory speed limit signs are posted on NY roads and highways to let motorists know what the maximum speed limit is in a certain area. These signs are white with black lettering. If no speed limit is posted then you may not exceed 55 mph. Many expressways also post minimum speed limit signs; usually 45 mph. Suggested speed limit signs are yellow with black lettering. These signs suggest to drivers that the road ahead may present a danger and that you should slow down. Always adjust your speed based on weather as well as road and traffic conditions. Be sure to maintain a following distance and continue to scan the road ahead with a good visual lead time.

SAFETY RESTRAINT SYSTEMS AND AIRBAGS

Safety belts have been proven to save lives in a variety of different collision situations. This is why California has a mandatory seat belt law. Every passenger in a vehicle 16 and under must be restrained as well as all passengers in the front seat. Drivers and passengers are responsible for the seat belt fine if they are over the age of 16 and in the front seat. Children age 4 and under must be restrained in a California approved car seat. There are exceptions for some children over 40 pounds who may not fit in a car seat. These children may use a properly installed booster seat.

Air bags in combination with seat belts provide the best protection for all front seat occupants. These bags usually go off at speeds around 10-12 mph. Nitrogen gas inflators ignite within a split second to surround front seat occupants providing them with an added layer of safety.

It is also recommended that the head rest is properly adjusted to the middle of your head. Make sure to also lock all the doors, since you are much more likely to survive the crash within your own vehicle. You are 25X more likely to be killed if thrown out of the car.

DISTRACTED DRIVING

Distracted driving has quickly become a major problem on our nation's highways. Taking your eyes off the road to check your mobile device presents a serious problem to both you and other drivers. California has now implemented a mobile device law. It is a traffic infraction to speak or listen to a hand held device while driving. You will also be fined and lose valuable license points.

Taking your eyes off the road for just 4 seconds is basically traveling the length of a football field with no vision. It is best to pack the cell phone out of sight and not use it at all while you are driving. If you must use it, pull safely off the road or in designated areas for mobile device use.

VEHICLE CONDITION

California requires all motorists to inspect their vehicles on a biennial basis. During this inspection, service technicians check your vehicles, smog protection, brakes, steering, lights and horn to make sure they are in proper working order. You should also make sure your tires tread depth meets the minimum standard of

2/32 of an inch of tread depth. It is also important to make sure your wind shield wipers are in good working order and that all the glass is clean especially the wind shield.

PRACTICE TEST QUESTIONS CHAPTER 5

1. Defensive driving involves which of the following skills?
   a. Visual lead time
   b. Following distance
   c. Staying alert and scanning with your eyes
   d. All of the above

2. Seat Belts reduce the severity of a collision when they are worn by:
   a. The driver and all passengers
   b. The driver only
   c. Passengers at high speeds
   d. Passengers on a long trip

3. Motor Vehicles must be inspected for smog in California :
   a. Every 5 years
   b. Every 2 Years
   c. If they break down
   d. Never, no inspection law in California

4. If no speed limit is posted, how fast can you drive?
   a. As fast as you want

b. 30 MPH
c. 45 MPH
d. 55 MPH

5. In what situation can you use a cell phone to text or email when driving?
   a. At speeds below 30 MPH
   b. On rural roads only
   c. In the city when you are stopped
   d. Never

6. The California Handbook recommends a minimum following distance of:
   a. 1 second
   b. 3 seconds
   c. 12 seconds
   d. 22 seconds

7. Collisions occur more often when:
   a. One car travels faster or slower than the speed of traffic
   b. The left lane is used for passing
   c. All cars are travelling at the same speed
   d. The flow of traffic is constant

8. When entering traffic from a complete stop or a curb you should?
   a. Drive slower than other traffic
   b. Leave a gap large enough to get up to the speed of traffic
   c. Accelerate quickly to get into the flow of traffic

d. Allow several cars to pass before entering traffic
9. It is illegal to leave a child unattended in a car at what age?
   a. 15 years old
   b. 12 years old
   c. 10 years old
   d. Age 6 and under
10. Seatbelts can prevent injuries but they also help you:
   a. Maintain control of your vehicle in a collision
   b. Stay trapped in your car
   c. Get thrown from your car
   d. Prevent injury In all side collisions

ANSWERS CHAPTER 5

1. A defensive driver maintains a good following distance, has a good visual lead time and constantly scans the road for problems (d).
2. Safety Belts are most effective when they are worn by the driver and all passengers (a).
3. Biennial inspections are required in California (b).
4. If no speed limit is posted then you may drive no more than 55 MPH (d). In cities this speed may be a lot less.

5. You may never use a cell phone to text or email when driving (d).
6. The California Handbook recommends a minimum of (b) 3 seconds following distance.
7. Collisions occur more often when one car travels faster or slower than the speed of traffic (a).
8. Leave a gap large enough to get your car up to speed (b).
9. It is illegal to leave a child 6 and under unattended in a car (d).
10. Seatbelts also allow you to maintain control of your car in a collision (a).

CHAPTER 6 ALCOHOL AND DRUGS

Driving under the influence of alcohol and drugs has always been a major factor in traffic fatalities across the United States. Tougher laws and increased awareness has made the situation better, however; impaired driving is still responsible for approximately 20% of traffic deaths in California.

Alcohol and drugs affects drivers in many different ways. One thing is for certain however; an impaired driver will make poor decisions, demonstrate lower inhibitions and will have reduced reaction times when dealing with a variety of traffic situations. Vision becomes especially restricted when driving at night. Recovering from the glare of a headlight becomes especially dangerous for an impaired driver.

BAC AND DRIVING

BAC or blood alcohol content is the amount of alcohol that is found in your blood after ingesting alcohol or drugs. The amount of alcohol in your bloodstream determines the level of intoxication which you can be charged for after driving impaired. In California State .08 is the presumptive level of intoxication for a DWI (driving while intoxicated). To put this in perspective, this number refers to approximately 4 relative size drinks for a 150 pound person in a one hour period. A relative size drink could be a 12 ounce beer at 4% alcohol, a 7 ounce glass of wine at 14% alcohol or a 1 ½ shot glass of hard liquor at 45%. Each of these drinks at these relative sizes is worth .02 on the BAC scale. Of course your weight and how much food you have in your stomach could alter these numbers. Experience with alcohol may change the way you react, but it will not change your BAC. When you combine alcohol with other drugs a synergistic effect occurs. In other words the drug will increase the effects of the alcohol.

It takes one hour to get rid of just one drink from your body. The liver is the organ that is responsible for filtering the alcohol from your body. It gets rid of about 90% of the alcohol. Breath and sweat account for the other 10%. It is also important to remember that your BAC continues to rise for one hour after your last drink. Taking a cold shower or drinking a cup of coffee just makes you a wet, wide awake drunk.

A DUI ARREST

Once you are administered a driver's license in the state of California you give your "implied consent" to submit to chemical test for the presence of alcohol. Refusal to take this test could result in an automatic revocation of your license. The three chemical tests that are admissible in court to be convicted of a DUI are the breathalyzer, a blood test or a urine test.

To decide whether you have been drinking and driving a police officer uses several tools in which to determine if you have been driving while impaired. They will first need a "probable cause" to pull you over. A probable cause could be anything such as driving too slow, driving too fast, swerving or perhaps even violating a traffic law. Once you are pulled over the officer will use observation to determine whether you have been drinking. They will look through your car as well as observe your manipulative skills as well as your speech. If they still suspect you have been drinking they may ask you to submit to a road side breath test and or a series of physical sobriety tests. If you are found to be intoxicated after the road side tests you will be arrested and taken to the police station to be administered one of the three tests previously mentioned.

The Penalties

A BAC reading of .08 or higher is a DUI in California. This is roughly four drinks in a one hour time period for an average size person. It is also illegal to drive in California with a BAC of 0.01% or higher, if the person is under 21 years old, or a BAC of 0.01% or higher at any age, if the person is on a DUI probation, or BAC of 0.04% or higher, in any vehicle requiring a CDL—with or without a CDL issued to the driver..

Besides fines and penalties many other consequences occur from driving drunk or impaired from the effects of alcohol and drugs. A judge may determine that you will have to install an ignition interlock device within your car. This device requires you to submit a breath sample before starting your vehicle. This device must be purchased and installed at the expense of the convicted driver. An open container of alcohol in your car can result in a fine, a surcharge, a victim assessment fee, possible jail time, as well as two points assessed to your driving record. If someone underage purchases alcohol their license can be suspended or it could possibly effect their ability to obtain a driver's license.

You may not carry liquor, beer, or wine inside a vehicle unless you are accompanied by a parent or other person as specified by law and the container is full, sealed, and unopened. If you are caught with an alcoholic beverage in your vehicle, the vehicle may be impounded for up to 30 days. The court may fine you up to $1,000, and either suspend your driving privilege for 1 year or require DMV to delay the issuance of your first DL for up to 1 year, if you are not already licensed. Your driving privilege will be revoked for 1 year, if you are convicted of either driving with a blood alcohol concentration (BAC) of 0.01% or higher or driving under the influence (DUI) of alcohol and/or drugs. On the first offense you will be required to complete the educational portion of a licensed DUI program. A subsequent offense may require a longer DUI program and you will not have a restricted DL to attend the DUI program.

ALTERNATIVES TO DRINKING AND DRIVING

1. Spend the night at a party and "sleep it off."
2. Use public transportation to get home.
3. Drink slowly and alternate non-alcoholic drinks to slow down intoxication.
4. Use a designated driver.
5. Call someone to pick you up.

PRACTICE TEST QUESTIONS CHAPTER SIX

1. What effect does alcohol have on your driving performance?
   a. Limits your recovery time from headlight glare
   b. Slows reaction time
   c. Effects judgment
   d. All of the above

2. How long does it take to oxidize a 12 ounce beer at 4% alcohol?
   a. One hour.
   b. Two hours
   c. One day
   d. 5 minutes

3. What is the presumptive level of alcohol intoxication for a DUI in California if you are 21 years old or more?
   a. .10
   b. .08
   c. .20
   d. .02

4. What happens if you combine alcohol with another drug?
   a. Nothing
   b. The combination of both can multiply the effects
   c. Only the medicine will affect your body
   d. The alcohol reduces the effects of the medicine

5. What practice insures safe driving after alcohol consumption?
   a. Take a cold shower
   b. Drink a cup of coffee
   c. Wait at least ten minutes after your last drink
   d. Call someone to pick you up
6. You give your consent to a test for alcohol consumption through your blood, breath or urine:
   a. If you are involved in an accident
   b. If you have been drinking alcohol
   c. Anytime you drive in the state of California
   d. If you receive a traffic ticket

7. At what BAC level does it become illegal for someone under the age of 21 to drive?
   a. .01 or higher
   b. .02.
   c. .08
   d. .16
8. What precautions should you take if you are using prescription or non-prescription drugs before driving?
   a. Check the warning label
   b. Consult your physician
   c. Wait for the effects to wear off before driving

d. All of the above
9. Which of the following drinks may be consumed while driving in a motor vehicle?
   a. Wine
   b. Scotch
   c. Beer
   d. None of the above
10. What constitutes probable cause to pull over a vehicle suspected of drinking and driving?
   a. Not wearing seat belts
   b. Swerving on the road
   c. Speeding
   d. All of the above

ANSWERS CHAPTER SIX

1. Recovery time from glare, judgment and reaction time are all effected (d).
2. It takes approximately one hour to oxidize one 12 ounce beer at 4% alcohol (a).
3. DUI in California is .08 or higher (b).
4. The combination of alcohol and drugs multiplies the effects (b).
5. Calling someone to pick you up is the best option (d).
6. You must comply with a test for alcohol anytime you drive in the state of California (c).

7. It is illegal to drive if your BAC is .01 or higher under the age of 21 (a).
8. You should take all of those precautions before driving on any drug (d).
9. You may never consume alcohol in a moving vehicle at any time (d).
10. All of the choices represent probable cause (d).

CHAPTER 7 SPECIAL DRIVING CONDITIONS & EMERGENCIES

Driving a motor vehicle is a very difficult task under normal conditions, but what are the proper procedures necessary in order to safely handle bad weather, night driving and emergency situations? A young driver needs to be prepared to meet a variety of driving situations including the complexity of high speed multi-lane freeway driving. Driving defensively means being prepared to meet every driving challenge

DRIVING AT NIGHT

When the sun sets driving a motor vehicle becomes even more difficult. Visibility is reduced drastically. This makes it very difficult to maintain a proper visual lead time. Your visual lead time now becomes the maximum distance that your headlights can project. Traveling faster than the distance that your headlights can project is called "overdriving" your headlights. It is important to decrease your speed at night, and to scan the driving path ahead as well as to the sides of the road with increased attention. Keeping your headlights and windshield clean will go a long way in keeping you safe at night. The law requires you to turn your headlights on thirty minutes before sunrise and thirty minutes before sunset. Low beams work much better in a fog situation. Be respectful when using your high beams. Be sure to use your low beams when approaching an oncoming driver. Their ability to see becomes not only their problem but also your problem.

HANDLING CHANGING WEATHER

Adding rain, snow or ice to an already complex driving task makes for a very dangerous situation. During a rain storm it is very important to "see and be seen." Turn your headlights on and drive in a position in traffic where you can be seen by other drivers. Increase your following distance and be aware of hydroplaning. Hydroplaning produces a very dangerous condition for all motorists. Be aware of increased pooling of water on the roads and slow down. Maintain proper tread depth on all four tires of your car as well as adhering to the manufacturers recommended inflation levels.

Similar to heavy rain, snow and ice produce very difficult driving situations. Once again it is important to drive in a position in traffic where you can see and be seen by other drivers. Remember to increase your following distance and to begin the braking process much earlier in order to avoid a skid. If a skid does occur remember to steer in the direction of the skid or more simply put, keep the front end of your car ahead of the back end. Prevention of a skid occurs long before you head out on your drive. Remember to clear all the glass in your vehicle of snow and ice thoroughly. Make sure the defroster, heater and fan are all set to the proper settings to help keep your windshield clean.

DRIVING EMERGENCIES

When handling any driving emergency it is important to follow the number one rule, don't panic. Being prepared for every type of emergency is equally important. Here are the procedures for handling some of the more common emergencies that you may be faced with:

Tire blowout/Loss of wheel- Hold the steering wheel tightly, take your foot off the accelerator and slow down gradually. Once your vehicle is under control, pull completely off the road and call for help. Should a skid occur handle it in much the same way you would in a winter emergency. Steer in the direction of the skid and try to keep your rear end ahead of the front end of your car.

Stuck accelerator- Try to hook your toe under the gas pedal and pry the pedal up. If this does not work, shift to neutral and use your brake to gain control of your car.

Headlight failure- Should your headlights fail, try using your directional signal, emergency lights or parking lights to help light your way. Get off the road safely and call for help.

Loss of brakes- If your brake pedal goes to the floor, and fails to stop your car, try pumping your brakes to build up pressure. If this does not help use your emergency brake. It is important to use slow steady pressure when using the emergency brake. Shifting to a lower gear will create "engine drag" and slow your car down more naturally.

Running off the pavement- If your wheels should go off the pavement, take your foot off the gas and slow the car gradually. Once the car is under control, steer gently back onto the pavement. If the shoulder is lower than the road, use the same procedure as above except you may have to steer at a sharper angle in order to return to the pavement.

Car approaching in your lane- Flash your lights and sound your horn to try and wake up a drowsy or impaired driver. It is also important to slow down and pull over to the right side of the road. Steering left could create a head on collision.

Stalling on a railroad track- Look and listen carefully to see if a train is approaching. If no train is in sight, shift your car to neutral and quickly try to push the car off the tracks. Should a train approach, abandon the car and walk toward the train to avoid being hit by the flying debris.

Expressway Driving

Driving on an expressway can be intimidating. Traveling at high speeds and through heavy traffic requires quick thinking and a well-planned defensive strategy. Isolating your vehicle can help alleviate many problems. The principle of isolation simply means to segregate your car away from other motor vehicles. A lot less can go wrong when there are fewer cars around you.

Entering the expressway may actually be the most difficult task when driving on fast paced multi-lane highways. It is important to identify a gap in traffic while you are on the entrance ramp. Once on the ramp get your speed up so that you can properly fit into that gap you have identified. Don't forget to signal your intention and to make a quick blind spot check before actually entering the freeway. Once on the freeway adjust your speed to the speed of traffic and isolate your vehicle.

Other special considerations to be aware of while driving at high speeds is to increase your following distance behind all vehicles, and to also increase your visual lead time to accommodate those higher speeds. Lane changing requires more of a "drifting" action as opposed to a quick "pull" of the steering wheel. Always remember to signal, check your mirrors and to check your blind spot before making any lane change. When exiting a freeway make sure to be in the proper exiting lane and to get into the deceleration lane as soon as it offered. Once on that ramp identify your new speed and adjust to the new speed limit.

PRACTICE TEST QUESTIONS CHAPTER 7

1. You press your brake pedal and nothing happens. What should you do?
   a. Pump the brakes to build up pressure
   b. Turn the key to off position
   c. Call for help
   d. Shift to neutral
2. What is a smart practice when entering an expressway?
   a. Stop on the ramp and wait for your gap
   b. Accelerate and let other traffic yield to your car

c. Enter the freeway slowly so other cars see you

d. Identify your gap early from off the ramp

3. When driving in fog you should
   a. Use your high beams
   b. Use your parking lights
   c. Drive without your lights
   d. Use your low beams

4. Your passenger side tires move off the pavement onto a gravel shoulder you should
   a. Slow down and steer gently back onto the road
   b. Brake firmly to gain control
   c. Accelerate and steer sharply onto the road
   d. Stop the car immediately

5. The number one rule in any emergency is
   a. Brake immediately
   b. Steer to the left
   c. Shift to neutral
   d. Don't panic

6. When are roads most dangerous during a rain storm?
   a. The first 5 minutes of the storm
   b. The last 5 minutes of the storm
   c. The middle of the storm
   d. Never

7. When driving at night it is a good practice to:
   a. Always use high beams
   b. Always use low beams
   c. Decrease your following distance
   d. Never drive faster than your headlights project
8. To help other drivers entering an expressway you should:
   a. Vacate the right lane
   b. Slow down
   c. Accelerate
   d. Put on your flashers
9. When driving in high winds it is best to:
   a. Reduce your speed
   b. Maintain two hands on the wheel
   c. Not use cruise control
   d. All of the above
10. If you are pulled over by a police officer you should:
   a. Drive to a rest area and pull over
   b. Pull off the left side of the road
   c. Stop immediately
   d. Pull over to the right shoulder when it is safe to do so

ANSWERS CHAPTER 7
1. When nothing happens when you depress the brake you should first try to pump the brakes to build up pressure (a).

2. It is best to identify your gap early to make it easier to blend with traffic (d).

3. Always use your low beams when driving in fog (d).

4. Get control of the car by slowing down when your wheels go onto the shoulder then steer gently back onto the road (a).

5. Don't panic is the number one rule when handling any driving emergency (d).

6. The first 5 minutes of any rainstorm are most dangerous because road oils are brought to the surface (a).

7. When driving at night you should not drive any faster than your headlights project (d).

8. Vacating the right lane will help oncoming drivers enter more safely (a).

9. When driving in high winds it is best to do all of the above (d).

10. If stopped by a police officer you should pull to the right side of the road when it is safe to do so (d.).

CHAPTER 8 SHARING THE ROAD

Believe it or not once you receive your license you will not be driving on the road with just cars. There are many other types of motorized vehicles as well as bicyclists, and pedestrians that you must be prepared to share the road with. Driving defensively and understanding the special rules necessary for all vehicles is extremely important. Their problem could become your problem if you are not sufficiently prepared to share the road with all road users.

TRUCKS AND LARGE VEHICLES

Trucks and large vehicles present many difficulties when driving on roads and highways. As a defensive driver it is always best to drop back and increase your following distance behind these oversize vehicles. Increasing your following distance does two things; it allows you to see the road ahead of the large vehicle as well as allowing this vehicle the ability to see you in their side view mirrors. Remember not all trucks can see you in their rear view mirrors.

Along with visibility problems large vehicles also require more time to stop, more room to turn, and more space to pass. It is important for us as drivers to understand these special needs. Remember that it is important to avoid driving in the blind spots of these large vehicles, and to make sure you follow the major defensive driving rule of "see and be seen." If a truck is passing you, slow down and allow them to pass, and then reestablish your following distance. It is a good practice to also keep plenty of space between you and large vehicles when they are behind you. Their massive size and weight requires much more time and space to stop when compared to a car. Make sure you signal all intentions early, and remember whenever you pass a large truck to be sure and see both of their headlights in your rear view mirror before returning to your original lane.

An oversize vehicle needs plenty of space when making a turn. Be sure to stop at the proper stop lines in cities and towns so that these trucks can complete their turns safely. Also understand that trucks will slow down when climbing a hill and speed up significantly on a downgrade due to their increased weight. When stopping behind any large vehicle be sure to leave plenty of space, especially on a hill. These vehicles need time to get going and may roll back slightly.

PEDESTRIANS AND BICYCLISTS

Pedestrians present a special problem. As a defensive driver you should always keep your eyes scanning for pedestrians as well as animals. Pedestrians have the right of way over vehicles at all times. Even a "jay" walking pedestrian has the right of way over a 2000 pound vehicle. It is your job to slow down and predict the worst at all times. Hopefully pedestrians will also obey the law and stay on the sidewalk as well as obey all of the traffic laws. Right of way laws also protect visually impaired pedestrians. They can be identified by a guide dog or perhaps a white cane. It is important that bicyclists obey many of the same rules that a motorist does. As a motorist you should always give other road users enough clear space when passing. Bicyclists must obey the rules of the road much the same way as motorists. If a bicycle lane is available they should use it. If there is none, they should remain as close to the right side of the road as possible so not to interfere with traffic. They should always come to a full stop before entering a main roadway from a driveway, curb or alleyway. Cyclists should also have an approved helmet as well as proper lighting, and reflectors to accommodate all conditions. They should also have adequate brakes as well as a horn or bell to alert other road users of their presence. Turns and stops should be indicated by using proper hand signals. A left hand turn is signaled by extending the left arm out in direction of turn. A right turn is signaled by a ninety degree left arm with fingers pointing to the sky. A stop is indicated a ninety degree angle with fingers pointed to the ground. Bicyclists should never carry a passenger and should have a least one hand on the handlebars at all times.

MOTORCYCLES AND OTHER SLOW MOVING VEHICLES

A defensive driver in a motor vehicle should always be on the alert for motorcycles. They can travel at speeds similar to cars, but they present increased visibility problems. Motorcyclists also have less protection and less stability. To increase their visibility motorcyclists should always drive with their headlights on and drive in a position in traffic where they can be seen by other drivers. They should wear approved helmets at all times as well as a face shield or goggles. Pass a motorcycle with care and sufficient space. Air pressure and wind can have a dramatic effect on their stability.

Mopeds are limited use motorcycles that travel at much lower speeds. The rules and licenses for these mopeds are based on the maximum speeds that they can attain. Higher speed mopeds will need to get a class M2 license while lower speed mopeds require any class of a driver's license. All mopeds are required to have a license plate and be registered. Mopeds normally drive in the right hand lane or on the shoulder. Class M1 higher speed mopeds may travel in any lane.

Tractors, postal vehicles and other slow moving vehicles should display a large orange reflective triangle. Use extreme caution when approaching all slow moving vehicles and have plenty of clear space when passing these vehicles.

PRACTICE TEST QUESTIONS CHAPTER 8

1. When no bicycle lane is available where should the cyclist ride?
   a. Facing traffic
   b. As far to the right of road as possible
   c. Middle of the lane
   d. As far left of the road as possible
2. When following behind a large vehicle it is a good practice to:
   a. Increase your following distance
   b. Speed up and get around the large vehicle
   c. Use your horn to let large vehicle know you are there
   d. Decrease your following distance
3. A visually impaired person has the right of way to cross the street when they:
   a. Are wearing sun glasses
   b. Are being helped by someone
   c. Are wearing light clothing

     d. Are helped by a guide dog and have a white cane
4. Motorcycles present a very specific traffic problem because:
     a. They are difficult to see
     b. They go too fast
     c. They don't have the same traffic regulations as cars
     d. They don't have to signal their turns
5. What does a slow moving vehicle symbol look like?
     a. It is octagon shaped and red
     b. A reflective orange triangle
     c. A red triangle
     d. Yellow and pentagon shaped

ANSWERS CHAPTER 8

1. A bicycle should ride to the far right when no bike lane is available (b).
2. It is always a good idea to increase your following distance for better visibility when following behind a large vehicle (a).
3. A visually impaired person has the right to cross the street when they have a guide dog and or a white cane (d).
4. Motorcycles can present a problem on the road because they are difficult to see (a).
5. A slow moving vehicle symbol is a reflective orange triangle (b).

Chapter 9 Road Sign Review

A   B   C   D   E   F

You will be expected to know and identify many of the signs that help make up the highway transportation system. In chapter one you learned that signs are divided up into one of four categories. Those categories are: Regulatory, Warning, Guide, Service and Recreation and

Construction. Take a look at the chart above and try to identify all the signs in each column, A-F. Also see if you know what category each sign belongs to. The answers are listed below.

ANSWERS CHAPTER 9
Column A

Stop Sign-Regulatory

Detour-Construction

Road Work Ahead- Construction

Detour- (version 2) - Construction

Pedestrian warning- Warning

No Parking- Regulatory

No Parking-(Version 2) - Regulatory

Column B

Parking Available- Guide, Service and Recreation

Dead End- Warning

Handicap Parking- Guide, Service and Recreation

No Parking-(Version 2) - Regulatory

Interstate Sign- Guide, Service and Recreation

Road Narrows- Warning

Column C

No Bicycles- Regulatory

No U Turn- Regulatory

Yield Sign Ahead- Warning

Yield Sign- Regulatory

End Construction- Construction

Two Directions of Travel- Warning

Column D

Under Construction- Construction

Wrong Way- Regulatory

One Way- Regulatory

Watch for Bicycles- Warning

Railroad Crossing- Warning

Speed Limit 55- Regulatory

Column E

Airport Ahead- Guide, Service and Recreation

Exit for City or Street- Guide, Service and Recreation

Construction Zone- Construction

Traffic Signal Ahead- Warning

State or County Road- Guide, Service and Recreation

Do Not Enter- Regulatory

Column F

Slippery When Wet- Warning

Tow Away Zone- Regulatory

Pedestrian Crossing- Warning

Exit Only- Warning, if the sign is green it is in Guide, Service and Recreation category

Curved Road Ahead- Warning

Men at Work- Construction

CHAPTER 10 PRACTICE PERMIT TEST

In this chapter you will take a practice permit written test. The test will contain questions from each section of the DMV Driver's Manual. Similar to the California Permit test it will include 46 questions similar to the ones you will encounter on your actual exam. After you have completed the exam, check your answers at the end of the chapter. Remember you need to get 38 or more correct to pass the exam.

46 QUESTION PRACTICE TEST

1. What must you do when you see a school bus stopped and its red lights are flashing?
   a. You may pass if the left lane is clear
   b. You must stop and wait for lights to stop flashing
   c. You may pass if no children are in sight
   d. You may pass if you are facing the school bus

2. What action should you take if you notice the traffic light has been green since you first saw it?
   a. Slow down and predict it will change to red

b. Speed up to get through light before it changes
c. Predict it will stay green
d. Check traffic quickly and speed up

3. Proper Defensive Driving involves:
   a. Correct use of your horn
   b. Scanning the roadway ahead and predicting the actions of others
   c. Predicting that other drivers will make up for your mistakes
   d. Looking straight down the road

4. Seat belts are most effective in preventing injuries if:
   a. They are worn by the driver only
   b. They are worn on short drives
   c. They are worn on long drives
   d. They are worn by the driver and passengers anytime they are in the vehicle

5. A vehicle has the right of way if it is:
   a. Already in a traffic circle
   b. Approaching a traffic circle
   c. Making a left hand turn
   d. Entering an expressway

6. How does alcohol affect driving skill and judgment?
   a. It only effects skill
   b. It only effects judgment
   c. It harms both skill and judgment
   d. It has no effect on skill and judgment

7. You may cross a single solid white line on a roadway:
   a. Anytime you want
   b. If you want to perform a u turn
   c. Only when performing a 3 point turn
   d. If traffic conditions require and it is safe to do so

8. If there are no sidewalks a pedestrian should walk:
   a. On the left side of the road
   b. Facing oncoming traffic
   c. With traffic
   d. On the side with the lightest traffic

9. When a motorist approaches a bicycle they should:
   a. Speed up and pass
   b. Slow down and give them space
   c. Proceed as normal
   d. Swerve into the opposite lane

10. What is the only true way to reduce your blood alcohol content (BAC):
    a. Take a cold shower
    b. Drink a cup of coffee
    c. Sweat the alcohol out
    d. Allow your body time to oxidize the alcohol

11. In California what BAC constitutes Driving Under the Influence (DUI):
    a. .12
    b. .02

c. .18

d. .08

12. Driving at night is more dangerous because of:

   a. Reduced vision

   b. Increased traffic

   c. Increase in pedestrians

   d. Increased speed

13. By law what vehicles must stop at all railroad crossings?

   a. Emergency vehicles

   b. Cars towing trailers

   c. Trucks

   d. School and passenger busses

14. This sign means   :

   a. Slow down and stop if you need to

   b. Come to a full stop

   c. Yield to oncoming traffic

   d. Proceed through the intersection without stopping

15. This sign means   :

   a. Always come to a full stop

b. Slow down only if an emergency vehicle is approaching
c. Continue through the intersection
d. Slow down and stop if necessary
16. What is the speed limit if it is not posted?
a. 65 mph
b. 45 mph
c. 55 mph
d. 35 mph
17. What is the best rule to follow in a driving emergency situation?
a. Don't Panic
b. Slam on the brakes
c. Speed up
d. Steer sharply to the left
18. If you pass your exit on the expressway you should:
a. Back up on the shoulder to your exit
b. Get off the next exit
c. Pull over and execute a three point turn
d. Do a u turn on the highway divider
19. When you combine alcohol with another drug it:
a. Reduces both effects
b. Has no effect on driving
c. Will reduce the effect of the alcohol
d. Can increase the effects of both

20. What will happen if you are under the age of 21 and are found to have a BAC of .01 or more?
    a. Your license will be revoked
    b. A two year jail sentence
    c. Your license will suspended
    d. No action will be taken
21. If your vehicle starts to lose control on wet roads (hydroplaning) you should:
    a. Immediately slam on the brakes
    b. Remain at the same speed and stay in your lane
    c. Slow down gradually and gently apply the brakes
    d. Pump your brakes
22. When Visibility is reduced the best action to take is:
    a. Slow down
    b. Clear your windshield
    c. Stop immediately
    d. Maintain current speed
23. In order to overcome the forces of inertia in a car it is best to:
    a. Pump your brakes
    b. Use all weather tires
    c. Wear your seat belt
    d. Stop your car
24. Which of the following constitutes a distraction while driving?
    a. Cell phone

b. Radio

c. Passengers

d. All of the above

25. Motorcycles present a safety risk to motor vehicles because:

a. Less likely to see in blind spots as compared to cars

b. They are less stable than cars

c. Drivers are more often not to see them

d. All of the above

26. In California children under the age of four must be restrained with a:

a. State approved child safety seat

b. Lap belt

c. Lap belt and shoulder harness

d. Automatic seat belt

27. When preparing to leave a curb you should:

a. Signal and enter traffic slowly

b. Wait for a break in traffic large enough to maintain speed of traffic

c. Wait for someone to let you in

d. Signal and accelerate into traffic

28. Blocking an intersection during heavy traffic is:

a. Is permitted if you are on a motorcycle

b. Is not permitted at any time

c. Is ok if you have the right of way

d. Is ok if traffic can get around you

29. You should increase your following distance when:
   a. You increase your speed
   b. When you follow large trucks
   c. When you cannot see well in front of you
   d. All of the above
30. Anytime you prepare to pass another vehicle you should:
   a. Put on your flashers
   b. Sound your horn to alert other drivers
   c. Accelerate quickly
   d. Signal, check your mirrors and check your blind spot
31. Roadway surfaces are most slippery:
   a. Before a rainfall
   b. First 5 minutes of a rainfall
   c. Middle of the rainfall
   d. At the conclusion of the rainfall
32. When a large truck begins to pass you it is best to:
   a. Slow down and allow truck to pass
   b. Speed up and get ahead of truck
   c. Change lanes and accelerate
   d. Stay alongside the truck
33. When parking your car on an uphill grade it is best to:
   a. Point your front tires away from curb
   b. Keep your tires straight

c. Point your tires anyway it doesn't matter

d. Point your tires into the curb

34. Traffic moving in the same direction is divided by:

a. Yellow lines

b. Red lines

c. Green lines

d. White lines

35. If you are under the age of 21 it is legal to drive with alcohol in the car:

a. If it is in the back seat

b. If bottle is half full

c. If a parent is in the car and it is unopened

d. If your passenger is holding it

36. If skidding occurs on wet pavement it is best to:

a. Speed up

b. Slow down and ease your foot of the gas pedal

c. Shift to a lower gear

d. Put your flashers on

37. When making a left hand turn from a one way street into a two way street :

a. Turn into the left lane

b. Turn into the center lane

c. Turn into the right lane

d. Turn into any lane

38. Which driving skills are impeded by the consumption of alcohol?
    a. Coordination
    b. Reaction time
    c. Alertness
    d. All of the above
39. A traffic light that has a red arrow pointing right means:
    a. You may not make a right hand turn
    b. Make a right hand turn after a complete stop
    c. Make a right turn anytime
    d. Turn right after checking for pedestrians
40. A U turn is allowed in a suburban neighborhood:
    a. If it is a one way road
    b. If it is a road separated by yellow double lines
    c. If a car is approaching
    d. When roadway is clear and it is safe to do so
41. After passing a vehicle it is safe to return to your original lane when:
    a. You can see both headlights of the vehicle you passed in your rear view
    b. You can see the front end of the car you passed in your side view
    c. Never
    d. Anytime you feel it is safe

42. The minimum drinking age in California is?
    a. 18
    b. 19
    c. 21
    d. 22
43. When driving in fog it is best to:
    a. Drive with high beams on
    b. Drive with no lights on
    c. Use your flashers only
    d. Drive with your low beams on
44. In the event of a brake failure the **first** thing you should do is:
    a. Pump your brakes
    b. Increase your speed
    c. Use emergency brake
    d. Shift to a lower gear
45. To warn drivers of a collision you should:
    a. Use flares to warn drivers
    b. Use reflective triangles to warn drivers
    c. Wave a flash light
    d. All of the above
46. If another driver exhibits road rage to you or your passengers you should:
    a. Scream back at them
    b. Speed up and get away
    c. Slow down and do not make eye contact with them
    d. Stare them down

Answers Chapter 10 Test

1. B- You must wait for the school bus lights to stop flashing
2. A- Slow down and predict it will change to red
3. B- Scanning the road ahead and predicting the actions of others
4. D- If they are worn by driver and passengers anytime they are in the car
5. A- Already in the traffic circle
6. C-It harms both skill and judgment
7. D-If traffic conditions require and it is safe to do so
8. B- Facing oncoming traffic
9. B- Slow down and give them space
10. D- Allow your body time to oxidize the alcohol
11. D- .08 is DUI
12. A- Reduced vision
13. D- School and passenger busses
14. B- Come to a full stop
15. D- Slow down and stop if necessary
16. C- 55 mph
17. A- Don't panic
18. B- Get off the next exit
19. D- Can increase the effects of both
20. A- Your license will be revoked
21. C- Slow down gradually then gently apply the brakes
22. A- Slow down

23. C- Wear your seat belt
24. D- All of the above
25. D- All of the above
26. A- State approved child seat
27. B- Wait for a gap in traffic large enough to maintain the speed of traffic
28. B- Not permitted at any time
29. D- All of the above
30. D- Signal, check your mirrors, check your blind spot
31. B- First five minutes of a rainfall
32. A- Slow down and allow truck to pass
33. A- Point your front tires away from the curb
34. D- White lines
35. C- If a parent is in the car and it is unopened
36. B- Slow down and ease your foot off the gas pedal
37. A- Turn into the left lane
38. D- All of the above
39. A- You may not make a right hand turn
40. D- When the roadway is clear and it is safe to do so
41. A- You can see the headlights of the vehicle you passed in your rear view mirror
42. C- 21
43. D- Drive with your low beams on
44. A- Pump your brakes

45. D- All of the above
46. C- Slow down and do not make eye contact with them

New California Laws 2018

Marijuana Use- It is illegal to smoke or ingest marijuana while driving or riding as a passenger on any road or highway in the state of California.

Motorcycle Training- Anyone 21 or older who wishes to ride a motorcycle in California will now have expanded training options.

Buses and Seatbelts- Effective July 1, 2018, it is required that a passenger in a bus equipped with seat belts to be properly restrained by a safety belt, except as specified. Parents, legal guardians, or chartering parties are prohibited from transporting on a bus, or permitting to be transported on a bus, a child who is at least 8 years old but under the age of 16 years old, unless they are properly restrained by a safety belt.

New DMV- Effective April 2018, DMV will begin offering an online driver license and identification application process. Applicants will have the opportunity to begin their electronic application before visiting DMV. Be sure to bring your application confirmation with you to your office visit.

OTHER BOOKS WEBSITE INFORMATION

You can get plenty of free information regarding all topics in the field of driver education by going to **www.driveredcoach.com**. On this website you can find valuable information on the latest driving techniques as well as important information to help you pass your road test.

I hope you found this book to be a valuable resource in your quest to secure a California driver's license. Hopefully the information you learned will carry over onto the California State roads and highways. My intention in writing this book was not only to help you pass the Permit portion of the California licensing procedure, but also to help you learn all the rules and laws that govern the California highway transportation system. It is also important for you to establish a critical partnership with your parents or guardians when setting up your practice driving sessions. I would strongly recommend that you seek out professional driving lessons either in a certified driver education program or through lessons with a private driving school. It will also be equally important for your parents or guardians to seek out the latest information regarding proper driving techniques and defensive driving skills. I have a couple of these books listed at the end of this chapter for a relatively low cost. .After all of these skills have been taught, and you feel you have reached a mastery level of knowledge, these critical skills you have learned must always continue to be reinforced throughout your driving lifetime.

As a way of expressing my thanks for your purchase, I am offering a FREE Guide to help you pass your road test. Just go to **www.driveredcoach.com** to claim your FREE Guide. Add your email to get special offers and updates on future publications and courses.

RECOMMENDED BOOKS TO HELP YOU LEARN HOW TO DRIVE THE CORRECT WAY:

"TEACH YOUR TEENAGER HOW TO DRIVE A CAR" SEQUENTIAL LESSONS FOR A NEW DRIVER

"SAVE YOUR TEENAGE DRIVER'S LIFE" IMPORTANT STRATEGIES TO TEACH A NEW DRIVER NOW!

THANK YOU
I hope you found "California Driver's Permit Practice Test Questions and Study Guide" helpful and will continue to use this as an

important resource regarding California driving rules and law. If you believed my book helped you in any way I would appreciate you leaving a short honest review on the Amazon Kindle website. This feedback will allow me to continue writing Kindle books that produce positive life changing results. Thanks again for purchasing and reading my book. Keep an eye out for future titles in the Driver and Traffic Safety field as well as several titles in the Health, Fitness and Wellness fields.

Made in the
USA
Columbia, SC